Prayers for Difficult Times

Prayers for Difficult Times

Conversations with God
about Things Often Left Unsaid

HELEN REICHERT LAMBIN

PRAYERS FOR DIFFICULT TIMES
Conversations with God about Things Often Left Unsaid
Helen Reichert Lambin

Editing Gregory F. Augustine Pierce
Design and typesetting by Patricia A. Lynch

Scripture texts in this work are taken from *The Message: Catholic/Ecumenical Edition*, © 2013 by Eugene Peterson. Used with permission of NavPress.

Copyright © 2017 by Helen Reichert Lambin

Published by ACTA Publications, 4848 N. Clark St., Chicago, IL 60640, (800) 397-2282, www.actapublications.com

Library of Congress Number: 2017931246
ISBN: 978-0-87946-588-9
Printed in The United States by Total Printing Systems
Year: 30 29 28 27 26 25 24 23 22 21 20 19 18 17
Printing: 10 9 8 7 6 5 4 3 2 First

♻ Text printed on 30% post-consumer recycled paper

Contents

Starting from Where We Are

Full disclosure here. I'll admit I don't pray nearly often enough, or consistently enough, or with enough focus. I tend to pray in fits and starts—particularly in fits, as when I'm having one about something. It is when life becomes more problem-shadowed that I am prompted to pray. It's not so much that I pray *for* something (although certainly I do that too), but rather it's a matter of my seeking *to* talk to Someone. Someone who is both one of us, but more, much more; Someone I trust and who understands and accepts me beyond comprehension; Someone who cares beyond human caring; Someone who is there, for me, even if nothing apparently changes—at least immediately—because of it.

People have been praying across centuries and across continents. They do it in words and in silence, in song and in art. They do it alone and as a community, at the happiest of times and at the most difficult of times. They do it because they were taught to, because it was a tradition in their family or tribe, and above all because they wanted and needed to do *something*. And what they have done, and still do, is pray.

The cave paintings at Lascaux, France, some 17,000 years old, could indicate a form of prayer for good hunting for food and a sign of respect for the animals that would become the food. Utensils and decorations buried with loved ones point to belief in a journey beyond—an act of hope and faith, conscious or unconscious, we still practice today. The Hebrew psalms, three thousand years old, are perhaps one of the best-known forms of ancient prayer. And yet reading them today can bridge millennia: prayers of love, grief, fear, joy, and thanksgiving; prayers for protection and forgiveness; and yes, prayers for destruction of enemies. (As far as the latter, as they say on TV occasionally, "Do not try this at home.")

Prayer has been defined in various ways. As I use here, it simply means talking with (whether out loud or silently) and waiting to listen to God (however you imagine the divine transcendent reality or mystery that transcends our rational selves), or perhaps it means just listening, without words of our own but receptive to whatever comes to us. But in both cases it is a conscious effort to "lift the mind and heart" to God, as it says in the Catholic catechism of my youth.

But prayer is a two-way conversation. There is Someone else there when we do it. In my case it is the God of the Christian faith, handed down to me from my family. But for others it is something else. There are different paths. Whatever God is, "it" is big enough to overcome our human brain's lack of comprehension and imagination. So, go ahead and pray in your own way and in your own tradition and take anything from this book that is helpful to you and leave the rest.

Sometimes it can be difficult to get "there" with prayer, wherever your "there" is. For that, scriptures and other holy writings from the various religious traditions can be a good jumping off place. Call it a leap of faith if you prefer. It can mean reading methodically or just reading along until something speaks to you: a chapter, a paragraph, a verse. Sometimes the spiritual reading inspires the prayer. Other times the prayer comes first and then we look for insight from others.

What amazes me in searching for the right words in the Bible is how often I can find ones that mirror what I'm feeling, what I'm thinking, what I'm agonizing over. Here are people who lived so many generations before me, in very different times and very different cultures, in distant places I've never seen and probably never will. And yet, back through the centuries, back across all those miles, is a bridge we can cross to share understanding of the God beyond understanding, the God who became part of human life.

Now let's have a word about the words *God* and *Lord*. When I am praying, I am not speaking theologically. I am calling out to the Almighty from the depths of my soul. What comes out of my mouth is both "God" and "Lord." So if you don't use either of those two words, substitute your own.

At the end of each of my prayers in this book, I have added a short quote from *The Message* by Eugene Peterson, a Presbyterian minister who has translated the entire Bible from the original ancient texts into contemporary American English. You may find this jarring at first, but if you give it a chance you will find it often makes familiar passages of the Hebrew and Christian Scriptures fresh and accessible to you.

At the end of each chapter, you will be invited to write your own prayer, in your own words and from your own starting point, about your own difficult times. The point is, prayer has to begin where you are. The concept isn't original with me, of course. It's been said often, but it is always surprising for me to rediscover. And so these are my prayers for my difficult times, which I share with you with some trepidation but in the hope that they might help you find your own prayers for yours.

Helen Reichert Lambin
Chicago, Illinois

PART ONE

Prayers for
Difficulty in Praying

TIMES OF DIFFICULTY IN PRAYER

The purposes of prayer are sometimes summarized as adoration, thanksgiving, oblation (offering up), contrition, and petition—or other words to that effect. Petition always comes last on this list, as if we're trying to sneak it in so maybe God won't notice. But asking God for something (even if it is only the word "help") is part of every personal prayer I pray and encouraged in group worship in the prayers for the community and others in need. The question that arises is: What is the purpose of the prayers for others and ourselves? If someone is alone or friendless, is God really going to say, "Too bad, you don't get healed, employed, loved, saved?" I asked that question of Fr. Carl Dehne, SJ, a retired theologian, teacher, preacher, spiritual director, and nursing home chaplain, as we walked along a street in St. Louis one day. His spontaneous answer was that petitioning God is the "divinization of the pray-er." That is, through asking God for something we are motivated and supported to share in God's work. I was so intrigued by the answer I that I simply stood in the middle of the sidewalk, trying to grasp it. Suddenly there was a huge clap of thunder and lightning flashed across the sky. Now that's what I call punctuation.

✣ Prayer for When You Can't Pray

Lord of Listening, how can I ask you to help me pray when I don't know how to pray any longer? It's like going in circles, since the act of asking for help in praying itself involves prayer. Last year I could pray like clockwork. Tic, tic, tic and I'm into the rhythm. Well, all right. It wasn't all that smooth and easy. But I could still do it well, at least most of the time. And I actually *liked* doing it. But now it's as though my capacity for prayer has somehow leaked away while I wasn't looking. Or while I wasn't praying. So I guess I have to leave it up to you, All Loving God. From my mouth to your ear. Now, what's that you're saying?

> *How gold is treated like dirt, the finest gold thrown out with the garbage, priceless jewels scattered all over, jewels loose in the gutters. (Lamentations 4:1)*

※ Spilled Words

Lord of Prayer, my words do not roll off my tongue with grace and poetry. There are those who can do so with poetry, and their words endure. Like the psalmists. Mine spill from my heart. They leak from the cracks and fault-lines created by sometimes breaking. Big and small. Here and there. So hear me, God of Wisdom, and help me listen to you. And, yes, allow me to remember that part of that listening is to keep up my part of the conversation—in my actions, in my words, but in your grace.

> ***Receive and experience the amazing grace of the Master, Jesus Christ, deep, deep within yourselves. (Philippians 4:23)***

※ Mostly Prayer

I'd like to pray more often that I do, God of Irony. But then come the distractions, like a herd of cats: things I'm worried about, excited about, mad about, glad about, forgot about; shopping lists, text messages to be returned, the car alarm down the street; or simply side trips of thought. With all that trouble and bubble, my words and thoughts turn to babble. So how do I quiet my mind and heart? Here you are, THE Transcendent Being who invites me into your company anytime I want, yet I can't focus. What emerges from me is a kind of Mostly Prayer, mingled with a lot of Muddled Me. I don't think I'm going to make it soon into Real or Pure Prayer. So if you'll settle for what I've got to offer, Approachable Lord, I'll keep on trying.

> ***If you seek God, your God, you'll be able to find him***
> ***if you're serious, looking for him with your whole heart and soul.***
> ***(Deuteronomy 4:29)***

❋ My Prayers and Scriptures

TIMES OF ATTITUDE

Attitude is a rather elastic word. It can be positive, meaning something like energy and confidence:"Let's have some attitude." It can be negative as in:"I don't like your attitude." ("And I don't like yours either.") It can be neutral or, rather, generic—meaning what the speaker wants it to mean or thinks it means. I see attitude as a kind of acted-out perspective. It is that which shows up in what I say or do and how I do—or don't—do it. It is my attitude that affects other people. And it is attitude that draws me closer to or farther from God.

�֍ Stiffened Spines, Not Necks

God of Strength and Gentleness, there are times, many times, when I am called to be flexible. There are times when I am called to lean into the prevailing winds. This is not one of those times. This is one when I need to stand firm, to stiffen my spine—and yet not become stiff-necked in the process, head turned away from your face. And I don't know if I am up to it, Lord of Acceptance. How am I to do this on my own? Or rather, how can we do this together? Help me to act with wisdom, courage, and honor. Remind me always that if I turn to you, you will be there with me, to sustain me with your divine grace.

> *Be brave. Be strong. Don't give up.*
> *Expect God to get here soon. (Psalm 31:24)*

Other People's Attitudes

Sometimes, Listening Lord, I get really annoyed with other people's attitudes. Not so much their actions, but their outlook. The one grows out of the other, doesn't it? And I think: How can they not see clearly what needs to be done? How can they not recognize the path to get there? How do we get them to listen? And maybe, harder still, how do I learn to listen to them? Because it's remotely possible that they don't like my attitudes and actions very well either. Teacher God, your Son, when he was among us, worked with such an ordinary, yet extraordinary in many ways, group of disciples. Guide me to work wisely and lovingly with both the ordinary and the extraordinary attitudes in my life.

> ***Were you listening in when God planned all this? Do you think you're the only one who knows anything? (Job 15:8)***

(Make) Room at the Top

God of Power and Humble Service, you give and welcome all our gifts. On those days when I'm feeling well supplied with a good attitude, and enjoying it, help me to remember to be grateful and, equally, graceful. For the moment, I may be sitting on top of the world—well, at least with a glimpse of the summit. But *your* summit isn't a narrow promontory. Rather, it's a vast plain or, better, a beautiful meadow where there is ample room for all. If necessary, remind me (gently, if you please) not to overdo it, but to leave space for others, their feelings and their concerns, and, yes, their attitudes and their gifts.

> ***His sacred mountain, breathtaking in its heights—***
> ***earth's joy. (Psalm 48:2)***

❀ My Prayers and Scriptures

TIMES OF DOUBT

There are people who never have any doubts about their faith. They have rock-bottom conviction and it stays solid. No major fissures. No high magnitude quakes. I'm not one of them. Sometimes I see my flame of faith burns brightly, giving both warmth and light. Sometimes it flickers and wavers like the candle I've carried in Easter Vigil processions. No matter how I try to shield it—cupping my hand, hiding it behind taller people, I'm afraid any moment it will go out. So what then? Possible plans: walk on in darkness; get back the light from someone else along the way; share my light with someone else along the way.

�֎ Gift and/or Grace

I didn't achieve it. I didn't acquire it. I probably sometimes don't even recognize it, God of Faith. I would say that it was a gift. Except that a gift is generally something you can do with what you want. And I think maybe this gift comes with some kind of user's guide. And there is another question. A gift often springs from love—but not always. Sometimes someone feels it is owed. But just what would it be that you owe me, Giving Lord? So maybe it's more like a grace. Or maybe it is gift and grace. Or maybe I just shouldn't try to define it in words. Don't get me wrong. However this gift/grace showed up, I'm glad to receive it. So how do I say—or show—my thanks? Or is that maybe part of the user's guide?

> *I'll give you a new heart, put a new spirit in you.*
> *I'll remove the stone heart from your body*
> *and replace it with a heart that's God-willed, not self-willed.*
> *I'll put my Spirit in you and make it possible for you to do*
> *what I tell you and live by my commands. (Ezekiel 36:26)*

❊ Spirit and Breath

What would I do without faith, God Hidden and Revealed? Whatever would I do? I have questioned it. Ignored it. Leaned on it. Played silly games with it. And taken it for granted like the air I breathe. When I think of being without faith, I feel...suffocated, as if I am at high altitude where the air is so thin that I gasp for breath. I think I'm suddenly beginning to understand, just barely, why your Spirit is called "the breath of life." I know I asked this before, and I know I'll need to ask it again...next year, next month, later today. But please, Faithful Lord, teach me how to nurture and care for the breath of faith.

> *God formed Man out of dirt from the ground*
> *and blew into his nostrils the breath of life.*
> *The Man came alive—a living soul! (Genesis 2:7)*

❊ Big Questions

We can't prove faith, Lord of No Proof. Or, for that matter, we can't really understand it or thoroughly explain it. That may have bothered me once, but not anymore. I don't really understand electricity, much less the Internet. Some physicist, God of the Universe, maybe a friend of yours (and maybe Richard Feynman), said: "If you think you understand quantum mechanics, you don't understand quantum mechanics. Maybe that's the same way with faith. So how can I expect to fully comprehend a transcendent God? The question I'm trying to figure out these days is how to live my faith in this world. Because that's the part that can be really hard.

> *So let's do it—full of belief, confident that we're presentable inside and out. Let's keep a firm grip on the promises that keep us going. He always keeps his word. Let's see how inventive we can be in encouraging love and helping out, not avoiding worshiping together as some do but spurring each other on, especially as we see the big Day approaching. (Hebrews 10:22-25)*

❀ My Prayers and Scriptures

PART TWO

Prayers for
Everyday Situations

TIMES OF DAY-TO-DAY SPIRITUALITY

When I was young and longingly looking forward to something and feeling frustrated by the days in between, my mother would say to me: "Don't wish your life away, Helen Irene. The ancient Romans had a saying: *"Carpe Diem,"* that is: "Seize the day." The difficulty in living in the present moment goes far back in the past. We haul a wagon full of yesterdays—good and bad. We push ahead of us a wheelbarrow full of tomorrows—worries, hopes, expectations, and unknowns. Small wonder it's hard to focus on *this* day. But this one, right here, right now, is what we have. By tomorrow it's gone, wherever old dreams and past days go. I still find myself counting the day or weeks until something difficult or unpleasant is over with or something special is going to happen. My mother has moved now beyond time to eternity, but I still now and then hear her reminding me: "Don't wish your life away."

✥ Tomorrow and Tomorrow and Tomorrow
Sometimes when I start to look ahead, Eternal God, panic: What if…? What might…? What will…? It's one thing if I can do something about it. Here and now. It's another when I can't. At least not here. At least not now. And maybe never and not at all. Sometimes it isn't easy to live with trust, Lord of Time, but I can't imagine how hard it'd be to live without it.

> *I'm absolutely convinced that nothing—nothing living or dead, angelic or demonic, today or tomorrow, high or low, thinkable or unthinkable—absolutely nothing can get between us and God's love because of the way that Jesus our Master has embraced us. (Romans 8:38-39)*

❀ Around and Around the Un-Merry Go Round

Round and round and round we go. Over the same ground. O, Lord of Ups and Downs, I don't know if I can't sleep because I keep going over and over and over the same things: things that I can't do anything about—at least not at this moment, especially not in the night hours. Or whether I keep going over and over and over the same things because I can't sleep. Can I not sleep because I'm so anxious? Or am I so anxious because I can't sleep? Never Exhausted God, remember that, even if I'm a grown-up, I'm still your child. Watch over me and help me fall asleep. And tell me gently, once again, to take things one day, or one night, at a time.

> *"Has anyone by fussing in front of the mirror ever gotten taller by so much as an inch? All this time and money wasted on fashion—do you think it makes that much difference? Instead of looking at the fashions, walk out into the fields and look at the wildflowers. They never primp or shop, but have you ever seen color and design quite like it? The ten best-dressed men and women in the country look shabby alongside them.... Give your entire attention to what God is doing right now, and don't get worked up about what may or may not happen tomorrow. God will help you deal with whatever hard things come up when the time comes."*
> *(Matthew 6:27-29, 34)*

❊ I Can Hardly Wait Until…

Patient God, I can hardly wait until tomorrow, next week, next month, next year. I want to finish this difficult project, get past a stressful time, arrive at that special occasion. I can't wait another minute to get through this day you have given me. How silly of me! I am wasting your most precious gift: time. Sure, I'm glad to have something to look forward to, but in the meantime here we are, Lord of Now, in this moment. What shall I make of it? I don't want to look back on this as "the day that got away."

> *This is the very day God acted—*
> *let's celebrate and be festive!*
> *Salvation now, God. Salvation now!*
> *Oh yes, God—a free and full life! (Psalm 118:25)*

❊ My Prayers and Scriptures

TIMES OF MISTAKES MADE (BY ME)

A recent way of offering apology without actually doing so (made popular among politicians and some religious leaders especially) is to say something like: "Mistakes were made." Passive voice. No actual subject. In other words, something went wrong somewhere, somehow, as a result of someone doing something, without anyone actually having to acknowledge that he or she has goofed up. It appears like an attempt to put a positive spin on a situation, except that while you're spinning you're really not doing much of anything else. There will be a positive spin in some of the prayers in this book, but first let me start by saying, loud and clear: "Mistakes (many) were made. By me."

✾ Lessons Un-planned

If part of experience is learning from mistakes, Lord of Experience, by now I should be thoroughly taught. I certainly have enough mistakes to my credit—or discredit. You would think that by now I ought to be some kind of pillar of wisdom. And yet, and yet, each time I make a mistake, you are there to help me try to pick up the pieces. You don't just shake your head, throw up your hands, and walk away. I'm thankful for that and I will continue to be thankful, as I make some of my same old mistakes...and some new ones, I'm sure. I hope, with your help, God of Constant Growth, to learn from them as well

> *Stalwart walks in step with God;*
> *his path blazed by God, he's happy.*
> *If he stumbles, he's not down for long;*
> *God has a grip on his hand. (Psalm 37:23-24)*

❊ Yes, No, and Maybe So

God of Practical Help, let me resolve one of the many flaws in my character causing me problems for the moment (actually for my lifetime to date). Teach me to distinguish, or better, to deal with two opposing tendencies: the impulse to give in or give up when I shouldn't, and the failure to yield ground when I should. Guide me to understand the difference between staunchly standing up for my principles and simply being stubbornly stiff-necked—and between trying to lead when I should follow and trying to follow when I should lead. Yes, Lord of Insight, now that I think of it, I have a lot of other opposing impulses, not to mention character flaws, I need to work on. But for now let's start with this one.

> *Never walk away from Wisdom—she guards your life;*
> *love her—she keeps her eye on you.*
> *Above all and before all, do this: Get Wisdom!*
> *Write this at the top of your list: Get Understanding!*
> *(Proverbs 4:4-9)*

❊ Obsessing or Blessing

Lord of Easy Forgiveness, I want to learn from all my mistakes—the ones I've already made and the ones I haven't made yet but surely will. But what I also ask is your help in my not obsessing about them. I cannot re-work history and perfect the past. And while you are at it, help me to extend the same favor to others, to help them not obsess about their mistakes— especially those that might involve me in any way. God of New Beginnings, I sometimes do wonder how in the world you put up with our silliness in thinking we will be perfect. Loving us as we are and fail to be is surely a sign of your love for all your children.

> *"I've loved you the way my Father has loved me.*
> *Make yourselves at home in my love. If you keep my commands*
> *you'll remain intimately at home in my love." (John 15:9)*

❀ My Prayers and Scriptures

TIMES OF GETTING MAD

It was said of the poet Lord Byron by Lady Caroline Lamb, his long-time lover, that he was "mad, bad, and dangerous to know." In this case the word mad meant more like "certifiably irrational." But it is no coincidence, I think, that the same word means "angry," as in "seriously p.o.'d." There can be good reasons for anger, and anger can be a force for change: sometimes for the better; often for the worse—in ourselves, in our families, in our workplaces, in our communities. And even when it does serve your justice, anger—like a swift-flowing river—has to be channeled and contained and must always leave room for forgiveness or reconciliation. Otherwise, like Lord Byron, we humans can become "mad, bad, and dangerous to know." It's better not to learn this the hard way.

✺ Mad at God

I would like to pray. I try to pray. I almost pray. But I can't. Can I say it? I'm too angry and upset with you, God Who Is Always Slow to Anger. (I hope that's true!) So now what? This is a time when I truly need you, even if I don't really want you around to rain on my righteous wrath. So don't go away. I know, I know, usually I come to you in awe and reverence. Sometimes you are even an old friend. But not today. Today that friendship is definitely strained. On my part, anyway. I know, I know: You've got plenty of things to be angry and upset with me about. But you're The Lord. I'm not. So don't go away, please. Okay?

> *All you saints! Sing your hearts out to God!*
> *Thank him to his face!*
> *He gets angry once in a while, but across*
> *a lifetime there is only love.*
> *The nights of crying your eyes out*
> *give way to days of laughter. (Psalm 30:4-5)*

Un-fair-grounds

Life isn't fair, Lord of Prodigal Generosity. Sometimes I think I deserve better from other people—at least on days like today when I was treated rather shabbily. Sometimes others treat me better than I deserve, and I'm grateful for that. And, yes, sometimes—maybe a lot of the times or too many times—they deserve far better from me. But today isn't one of those days. I'm the aggrieved party today. God of Mercy, guide me to learn from and grow from these times when others are less than fair to me. And give me the grace, wisdom, and courage to help make life fairer for them the rest of the time!

> ***"You're blessed when you can show people how to cooperate instead of compete or fight. That's when you discover who you really are, and your place in God's family." (Matthew 5:9)***

The Nightly News

God of Earned Trust, I'm upset again. I was watching the evening news, getting mad at the stories of injustice, violence, deprivation, destruction, you name it. I've seen lots of good in your world. But too many news nights I see the frightening footprints of evil, of greed, of indifference, and the stray wandering footprints of ignorance and venality. So, Leader Lord, protect us from naiveté, cynicism, and passivity. Let us experience a dose of *metanoia*, a change of heart, when needed. And maybe sometimes we need a healthy modified Damascus experience in the manner of St. Paul. Sometimes being knocked off our high horse can be a helpful lesson.

> ***"You're blessed when you get your inside world—your mind and heart—put right. Then you can see God in the outside world." (Matthew 5:8)***

❁ My Prayers and Scriptures

TIMES OF ABSENCE

There is a well-known saying about love: "Absence makes the heart grow fonder." But there are many difficult times when absence is the problem that must be prayed about. It may be when a child has gone off to college or the military or simply left home to pursue a job or career or married to start a new family. Or it may be when a good friend has moved to another state or simply found other interests that do not include you. Or it may be the ultimate absence of all: the death of a loved one. Maybe this doesn't apply to other people, but I know that the absence of someone I love certainly complicates things for me with God. There may be people who never feel that God is off to some other section of their universe, tending to others who are more favored, more deserving, more in need than me. I admire those unwavering believers, but I am not one of them. I waver—quite a lot. For me, oddly enough, out of these times of absence there comes, little by little, a new experience of the divine presence. So, yes, I'd definitely rather do without absence. And yet, I'm beginning to learn that absence can make the heart grow fonder—God's absence included.

✻ Prayer and Presence

Help me to sense your presence, God of Accompaniment, as I mourn in prayer the absence of a loved one I am experiencing. I don't ask for some kind of miraculous change in our situation. In fact, I need to learn to accept it. But I need to be able to tell you how sad I am feeling. Teach me, Lord, to remain in your presence and allow it to comfort me. Keep my loved one safe and help us remain in contact, O Lord Who Is Always Both Far and Near.

> *Send for some singers who can help us mourn our loss.*
> *Tell them to hurry—*
> > *to help us express our loss and lament,*
> *Help us get our tears flowing,*
> > *make tearful music of our crying. (Jeremiah 9:17-18)*

❈ Missing Persons

I miss talking with you, Listening Lord, now that we're not speaking. At least, I'm not speaking to you, because I feel you have not heard me when I so needed to be heard about the loss of my loved one. It's not easy. All the words, all the feelings, all the lamentations. I used to bring them to you, but it feels as if you have left me too. Where shall I take them now? I'm all dressed up in my rather shabby robes of mourning, with no place to go. We need to get back together, Lord. To pull our friendship—if it's all right to use that word—back where we left off. But I don't know that I'm able to take the first step, God of Receptivity. Could you? Would you? Or maybe, if I'm asking this, you already have.

> *"I've made myself available*
> *   to those who haven't bothered to ask.*
> *I'm here, ready to be found*
> *   by those who haven't bothered to look." (Isaiah 65: 1)*

❈ Room with a View

God of Comfort, let it be as if we were each in comfortable chairs in a comfortable room. Maybe one with a view. We don't even need to talk. Unless you want to. Maybe otherwise we could just sit there in companionable silence for a while. And then, before I leave, maybe you could give me some direction about what I'm supposed to do when I leave the tranquility of this room. How do I take your presence with me and use it to accept the absence of my loved one? I know it's lot to ask, me being who I am, and you being who you are. Then again, with you being the Lord Who Is Always There for Me, maybe it's not.

> *"Let me give you a new command: Love one another. In the same*
> *way I loved you, you love one another. This is how everyone will*
> *recognize that you are my disciples—when they see the love you*
> *have for each other." (John 13:34-35)*

❦ My Prayers and Scriptures

PART THREE

Prayers for
Special Situations

TIMES OF THE DARK NIGHT OF THE SOUL

The Heart of Darkness is the title of a novel by Joseph Conrad about the evils of European colonization in Africa. St. John of the Cross wrote of the "Dark Night of the Soul." Both titles speak to me at really difficult times. Scripture also uses multiple images of light and darkness, especially in the Gospel of John. These images seem to speak to anyone who has experienced profound loss and grief, which I have many times. Heart. Darkness. Our faith tells us that, yes, there is ultimately light at the end of the tunnel, but experience also tells us that to reach it you have to go through the darkness. And that can be a difficult journey indeed. Denying it simply diminishes the dignity; it doesn't shorten the journey. But we don't have to make it alone. God is present with us, whether we call or not. "*Vocus atque non vocus Deus Aderit*," Carl Jung had carved in Latin over his front door when he was alive and on his gravestone when he died. "Bidden or not bidden, God is present."

Slogging Along

God, Creator of Stars and Constellations and Galaxies and maybe Universes, how do I find light in this darkness? Enough, anyway, to find my way? How long do I have to wait? What do I have to do? Do I slog along patiently, one foot after the other, hour by hour, day by day? Is there a faster, better way? How long, O Lord of Good Results, before I see some light?

> ***Jesus once again addressed them: "I am the world's Light. No one who follows me stumbles around in the darkness. I provide plenty of light to live in." (John 8:12)***

※ Hands

Lord of Complete and Total Wisdom, I don't want to be presumptuous, but sometimes you really need to hold out your hand to us. If we can't quite reach it or don't quite see it, can't you in due season reach out a little further, and a maybe little further still? And God, O My God, this is one of those times. Oh yes, this is one of those times. And maybe I should ask this also: For those times when it is my turn to reach out to others experiencing the darkness, guide and strengthen my hand, and let me be a light unto them.

> ***"I, your God,***
> ***have a firm grip on you and I'm not letting go.***
> ***I'm telling you, 'Don't panic.***
> ***I'm right here to help you." (Isaiah 41:13)***

※ Unpaired Prayer: Pass It On

Were things really so different once, Unchanging God? Was loving someone and being loved by someone really something so *everyday*? I can remember *loving* my beloved, but it's so hard to hold on to the feeling of being loved in return. Lord of Love, when I was half of that so special *we*, it was so much easier for me to be generous of spirit. I could feel so much more love to others because I felt so loved. Now it's *me* and not *we*, and sometimes, lots of times, it's so much harder to be nice. Not phony nice, but nice in the best sense of the word. Remind me again, Lord of Relationship, that you always love me, so that I can remind myself to pass it on to your other children whom you love just as much.

> ***You're here to be light, bringing out the God-colors in the world. God is not a secret to be kept. (Matthew 5:14)***

❋ Showers and Tears

God of Sorrow, your Son wept for his friend Lazarus. My sorrow sheds tears that fall invisible, tears I cannot shed. Let them fall as quiet rain. Not now the thunder and lightning. Bring gentle rain water to this bleak barren soil within me. Let my thirsting heart drink from your well.

> *"Open up, heavens, and rain.*
> *Clouds, pour out buckets of my goodness!*
> *Loosen up, earth, and bloom salvation;*
> *sprout right living." (Isaiah 45:8)*

❋ My Prayers and Scriptures

TIMES OF DIVINE ABANDONMENT

F. Scott Fitzgerald wrote. "In the real dark night of the soul it is always three o'clock in the morning." Rose-colored glasses can be lovely, but not if worn constantly. It's difficult when bad things or hard things—and sometimes there's a difference—happen to us. It is, perhaps, even more difficult when they happen to others we love. Sometimes, as a wise friend said to me, we can only listen and love. And as I grow older—careful, I did not say "old"—I am learning that it can be hard when bad things or hard things happen to people we don't even know. People in our own world. People half a world away. We all feel abandoned, left to our own devices, and that's a good thing, because far worse, it seems to me, is when we cease to care.

How Do I Trust?

How do I regain my trust in you, Lord of the Abandoned? I thought we were friends. I called you Parent God. I thought you were all powerful. But you let this terrible thing happen. Couldn't things have been different? Couldn't you have prevented it? Or are there some things even you can't do or prevent? How do I pray to you now? Who are you? Where were you? Where, tell me where, was the palm of your hand?

> ***Trust God from the bottom of your heart;***
> ***don't try to figure out everything on your own.***
> ***Listen for God's voice in everything you do, everywhere you go;***
> ***he's the one who will keep you on track. (Proverbs 3:5-6)***

❋ Detachment 101

So many losses, God Who Leads the Lost, in my life, among my friends, in my community, in my world. I'm afraid to care. Or fear I care too much. What if…? What if…? What if…? I have even asked you, Lord of Redemption, let me learn to stop caring so much. Let me learn to be more detached. But either I'm not asking for the right thing or your answer isn't what I begged for. Because I keep right on caring. So much for detachment. So instead, please give me grace to act wisely on my caring.

> *"You're blessed when you're at the end of your rope. With less of you there is more of God and his rule. You're blessed when you feel you've lost what is most dear to you. Only then can you be embraced by the One most dear to you." (Matthew 5:3-4)*

❋ Grief Offering

Gracious God, how do I, how can I, help others now, in my own time of pain and desolation? It's bad enough to feel such sadness. It's worse if there is no point to it at all. Can I offer my pain to you, Lord of Light-from-Darkness, as a prayer itself? Let my grief become a prayer rising, like rough incense, for myself and for those I love, for those who love me, and for those who long to be loved.

> *God, come close. Come quickly!*
> *Open your ears—it's my voice you're hearing!*
> *Treat my prayer as sweet incense rising;*
> *my raised hands are my evening prayers. (Psalm 141:1-2)*

❁ My Prayers and Scriptures

TIMES OF HOPE DEFERRED

Hope is the thing with feathers
That perches in the soul,
And sings the tune—without the words,
And never stops at all.

Emily Dickinson

Emily Dickinson usually wore a white dress, rarely if ever left her house in Amherst, and may or may not have suffered from unrequited love. But she could write with beauty, and she got "hope" right. It is a thing with "feathers" that "never stops at all." Hope gets sort of short shrift (that's an Iowa phrase) in our relationship to Scripture. It's one of the big three in Paul: faith, hope, and charity (see 1 Corinthians 13:13), but we don't hear a lot about it as we do, for example, faith—or love, which is the biggest of Paul's big three. We may hope to grow in love and live our faith. But how many times do we talk to ourselves gently—or sternly—about growing in hope? I know I tend take it for granted when I have it and ignore it when it gets weak. I certainly won't argue about the importance of love and faith, but I also think that, without hope, faith and love become very difficult to practice—or maybe even feel. So here's to hope! If it's strong, salute it; if it's more fragile, nurture it; and always embrace it.

❈ Together

God of Hope, I don't expect to avoid heartbreak my entire life. Your Son certainly didn't. He had many times of pain and grief. This is why I can come to you now in this time of Hope Deferred. Jesus must have had hope in carrying out his mission, even when things looked bleak, even in those terrible days of his passion and death. Was he ever tempted to just throw up his hands and say: "That's it, Father. I think we need to rethink this entire plan." I am in one of those times when it's really hard to hold on to hope. Just be with me, Lord of Comfort, and let me know you are always there.

> *The moment we get tired in the waiting, God's Spirit is right alongside helping us along. If we don't know how or what to pray, it doesn't matter. He does our praying in and for us, making prayer out of our wordless sighs, our aching groans. He knows us far better than we know ourselves, knows our pregnant condition, and keeps us present before God. That's why we can be so sure that every detail in our lives of love for God is worked into something good. (Romans 8:26-28)*

❈ Hope Is in the Air

Maybe something good will happen for me this day, this week, this month, this year. And if it isn't happening yet, I feel it in the air, like a spring breeze. All Knowing Lord, this has been a hard time for me, a time of feeling down and defeated, but I am not yet finished, still less forgotten. But for this moment, God of All Possibilities, let me welcome and enjoy a gentle breeze of hope. Or, if you will, the wind of your Spirit.

> *Oh! May the God of green hope fill you up with joy, fill you up with peace, so that your believing lives, filled with the life-giving energy of the Holy Spirit, will brim over with hope! (Romans 15:13)*

✿ Thankfully Hopefully

Thank you. Thank you. Thank you, God of Promise, for the gift of hope. I'm not talking now about my Overly Great Expectations or your assurance that everything, everyday, from here on out will be Smooth Sailing. My rose-colored glasses are more like bifocals, with plain glass set in the frame as well. But after a time when hope—that "thing with feathers," as Emily Dickinson described it—seemed to fly right past my head, now it's back, perched—hopefully—in my soul. I don't want to frighten it off, so I'll treat it gently, O Lord of Giving Only Good Things, but how welcome it finally is!

Believe in God, and he'll help you recover. Invest your hope in him and he'll lead the way. Respect God and expect one beautiful friendship. (Sirach 2:6)

✿ My Prayers and Scriptures

_____

_____

_____

_____

_____

_____

_____

_____

_____

_____

_____

_____

_____

_____

_____

_____

TIMES OF CREATING A REAL MESS

All mistakes and mess-ups are not created equal. There are minor ones that happen all the time. Medium versions that come once or twice a year, if we're unlucky. And then there is "I really messed up." These are the mistakes in judgment and action that we don't just put neatly behind us and vow never to make again. These are the real messes that are behind us, beside us, and in front of us. We slog through them, step by stumbling, questioning step. Dawn is very distant and often very dim. All that slogging does lead somewhere. It leads us to prayer. The very point of redemption is that there is something we need to be redeemed from, and only God can do that for us.

✿ Beyond Mistakes

Lord of Forgiveness and Redemption, I cannot believe I did something that stupid, selfish, insensitive—just plain wrong. It's out of character for me. Really. You know that. Other things I do that are stupid, selfish, insensitive, and just plain wrong are, unfortunately, in my character. But this one, no. Why didn't you stop me? Or rather the question is: why didn't I ask for your help *before* I made the mess? Wisdom God, who so patiently appears to suffer fools (like me) gladly, even willingly, help me (and all of my sometimes fellow fools) to ask first—instead of after—for your guidance next time. And please help me get out of this mess!

Change your life, not just your clothes.
  Come back to God, your God.
And here's why: God is kind and merciful.
  He takes a deep breath, puts up with a lot,
This most patient God, extravagant in love,
  always ready to cancel catastrophe. (Joel 2:13)

✺ Mess and Meaning

Is it possible, God of Salvaging, to draw some redemptive meaning out of the mess—or messes—I've managed to make of things? If so, what is it that I need to do? Wishing I had *done* better can be a good kick in my…soul… to try to do better in the future, but I think, I hope, I feel that there's an important lesson I'm supposed learn from this fiasco. The trouble is, I don't know what that lesson is. Lord of Infinite Second Chances, without trying to turn this mess I made into some kind of "cheap grace"—or a kind of smug denial of my responsibility for it—how do I find the meaning in this mess? (Did I mention that I know it was my own fault?)

> *Count yourself lucky, how happy you must be—*
> *you get a fresh start,*
> *your slate's wiped clean.*
> *Count yourself lucky—*
> *God holds nothing against you*
> *and you're holding nothing back from him. (Psalm 32:1-2)*

✺ My Prayers and Scriptures

_____

_____

_____

_____

_____

_____

_____

_____

_____

_____

Time of Surviving the Unsurvivable

I have not watched much of the popular "survivor" series on television. I always figure that real life, everyday life, has more than enough challenges without having to manufacture them. And made-for-TV survivors don't impress me anyway. What is impressive is when real people who have undergone horrific experiences, encountered disaster (human-made and natural), endured real and often unforeseen heartbreak, or faced true evil emerge—not unscathed but able to go on with their life. Even more amazing is when some of us grow from our experience and become people of compassion, people of integrity, people with gifts, people with promise. True survivors.

🦋 Wounded Innocence

God of Countless Tears, today in the news was yet another story of childhood innocence fractured by a sexual predator. Only the victims can know the true nature of the pain—physical, emotional, spiritual, psychological. Not even those of us who know them personally or love them from afar can remove even part their pain from their shoulders. But you can, Lord of Survival. In your Son's life among us, he was an innocent victim, a "lamb to the slaughter," as Isaiah says. He healed the sick and brought hope to the survivors of unspeakable acts. Send your Spirit to them now. Help the victims become survivors and maybe even someday join the ranks of "wounded healers" themselves.

> *"I'm calling a meeting, Jacob.*
>> *I want everyone back—all the survivors of Israel.*
>> *I'll get them together in one place—*
>> *like sheep in a fold, like cattle in a corral—*
>> *a milling throng of homebound people!*
> *Then I, God, will burst all confinements*
>> *and lead them out into the open.*
> *They'll follow their King.*
>> *I will be out in front leading them."* *(Micah 2:12-13)*

✿ Why…and How?

Lord of Life, when I've come face to face with profound suffering, I've asked you *Why? Why?* Suffering among those close to me, or known to me, or at a distance among those I'll never know. And, yes, on a few occasions, *why me?* I don't suppose I'll give up asking this tiny question, but maybe the question instead should be *How? How?* How could some people so wounded grow from their unbearable experiences to become stronger, wiser, kinder, more creative, and more compassionate? How did they become no longer *victims* but *true survivors*, survivors who bring their own light to others? God of Survival, help all of us who face times of terrible pain and enveloping darkness feel your love and grow with your always available grace.

> *Though the cherry trees don't blossom*
> *and the strawberries don't ripen,*
> *Though the apples are worm-eaten*
> *and the wheat fields stunted,*
> *Though the sheep pens are sheepless*
> *and the cattle barns empty,*
> *I'm singing joyful praise to God.*
> *I'm turning cartwheels of joy to my Savior God.*
> *Counting on God's Rule to prevail,*
> *I take heart and gain strength.*
> *I run like a deer.*
> *I feel like I'm king of the mountain! (Habakkuk 3:17-19)*

✳ Survivor School

I don't know that I should or could call myself a survivor, God of All Who Suffer, considering what has happened to others in this fragile world. But, yes, there are things I have survived over the years: loss of loved ones, financial anxiety, temporary disability. And, yes, I have survived the good parts too: the truly good parts and the parts that only seemed good at the time. Still, I have the feeling I should have done more with your gift of survival. So again I have a question for you, Lord of Answers: What is it I should learn today from having survived what I assumed at the time was unsurvivable?

> *I ask—ask the God of our Master, Jesus Christ, the God of glory— to make you intelligent and discerning in knowing him personally, your eyes focused and clear, so that you can see exactly what it is he is calling you to do, grasp the immensity of this glorious way of life he has for his followers, oh, the utter extravagance of his work in us who trust him—endless energy, boundless strength!*
> *(Ephesians 1:17-19)*

✳ My Prayers and Scriptures

_____

_____

_____

_____

_____

_____

_____

_____

_____

TIMES OF DEEP DEPRESSION

This is the section of prayers I really don't want to have to write. I don't like remembering my bouts with serious depression. On April 4, 2010, Easter Sunday night, I fell down the back steps at bedtime, letting out the small dog we had adopted just seventy-five days earlier. It was my fault, not the dog's. It was rainy and slick, and I was relaxed, hurried, and inattentive after good food and good wine with family and friends. In the fall I broke my humerus. (No, it definitely wasn't humorous.) My options were to wear a brace for about three months or have surgery and have a rod and pin installed. I opted (initially) for the brace to avoid surgery. So for eleven weeks I wore this big beastly plastic brace that came up to my shoulder, down to near my elbow, and strapped across my chest, under the arm, and across the back to the left arm. Much of what I had always been able do in my usual, ordinary, everyday life I could no longer do. Among them, I couldn't write, drive, garden, knit, or shower properly. And the little I could, I didn't want to. Because the other thing I fell into, that rainy Easter Sunday night, after the fall, was a full-blown depression. It was, in my judgment now, reactive rather than chronic depression. During the time in the brace, I wrote in a notebook a series of prayers—I couldn't type them on the computer. They were—in total—the bleakest, darkest prayers I have ever prayed or written. Prayers of despair, defeat, desperation…and guilt because I also thought that among other things this was punishment for things done, things left undone, and for basically being me. Which added to the poisonous stew. Eventually, I even ran out of prayers. Later, when this period was over, I considered destroying those prayers. But instead, I decided to include some of them here. My depression did not last forever, and I hope yours will not either These are prayers for anyone who has ever needed bleak, dark prayers. Instead of titles below, I have included dates I wrote the prayers. Eventually I had the surgery anyway, because by June of 2010 the bone still wasn't completely healed. So I had the rod and pin installed in the bone and became in part a bionic woman. The surgery was followed up by months of physical therapy, but the depression finally lifted. The last prayer below was written recently.

❋ Depression Prayer April 21, 2010

Lord of the Hopeless, I am so depressed I can't stand it. I am tempted to write: "I wish I were dead." I don't know if I mean it, but it's close. I feel utterly hopeless and helpless. Time that used to fly for me, drags endlessly, with no moments of joy or hope to lighten the burden of my days. I am terrified that I will never be well again, walk the dog with confidence, work in the garden, travel alone or with others, or ever be the person of confidence and competence I once was. Help me, God All Powerful, help me. I know other people experience much worse things than I am experiencing now, but still I am truly in despair.

>*And you, Jeremiah, will say this to them:*
>*"My eyes pour out tears.*
>>*Day and night, the tears never quit.*
>*My dear, dear people are battered and bruised,*
>>*hopelessly and cruelly wounded." (Jeremiah 14:17)*

⁂ Depression Prayer April 25, 2010

God of Pain, I know I needed to learn a lesson about compassion for the emotionally distraught. And I have learned, Lord, or at least I am learning. But if the learning destroys me through despair, how does that help anything? Is this simply punishment for some wrong I did, real or imagined? My own hell of my own making? Nearly three weeks now since my accident and I am still in the depths of depression. It is worse, in a way, than the terrible days after my husband's death. Then, at least, I could act, move, take charge, even hope, with some kind of certainty, that time would bring some healing. Lord of Compassion, lift this cloud of darkness from me, little by little, even day by day. Show me a way to get through this, Lord; hold out your hand and I'll grasp it.

> ***Open up before God, keep nothing back;***
> ***he'll do whatever needs to be done:***
> ***He'll validate your life in the clear light of day***
> ***and stamp you with approval at high noon. (Psalm 37:5-6)***

⁂ Depression Prayer April 28, 2010

Lord of I Can't Wait Any Longer, when will times get better for me? So far, there is little let-up in my depression, and I am beginning to think I'll never get better. I am suddenly afraid that I am having a mental breakdown, afraid something else bad will happen to me or to one of my loved ones. Instead of getting easier, things just seem to be getting more complicated and more depressing. Absent God, I need you now. Something has to give before I do. Why don't you answer my call?

> ***God, are you avoiding me?***
> ***Where are you when I need you? (Psalm 10:1)***

❀ Depression Prayer May 6, 2010

I am broken, God of Wholeness. I am broken in body, in spirit, in heart. Day by day I should be growing stronger, but I am terrified that I will never truly heal. To you, I pour out my fear and sorrow and sense of loss. I am so terribly homesick for the life I once had. I felt then like a tough old girl. Now I feel more like a fragile little old lady. Please, Lord of Mental Health, help me. Hold me in the palm of your hand and sustain me and heal me of my brokenness. Protect me, O Lord. I am trying to hang on.

> *Jesus, overhearing, shot back, "Who needs a doctor: the healthy or the sick? I'm here inviting the sin-sick, not the spiritually-fit."*
> *(Mark 2:17)*

❀ Depression Prayer 2016

Extraordinary Lord, I thank you from the bottom of my heart for my "ordinary" post-depression days. I give thanks for waking up to a lovely spring rain and looking forward to a little spring planting. For being able to go grocery shopping and book browsing. For being able to go to church and sit in a wooden pew. For my family and friends that went through my depression with me. For your presence that helped me through those dark days, even when I could not always perceive it. I now know that depression can visit any of us at any time and that some people cannot seem to ever overcome it. I pray especially for them.

> *River fountains splash joy, cooling God's city,*
> *this sacred haunt of the Most High.*
> *God lives here, the streets are safe,*
> *God at your service from crack of dawn. (Psalm 46:4-5)*

❋ My Prayers and Scriptures

TIMES OF DEMENTIA

Sometimes it has been called "second childhood." The term referred to adults whose cognitive capacities have become so diminished so that in time they began to require the kind of care and supervision given to children. Now it is called "dementia." A form of dementia is caused by Alzheimer's Disease. The term "second childhood" sounded kind and was probably kindly meant. But it's a misnomer. Children grow into the fullness of who they are. Experiencing it and watching it is a happy thing. Dementia is not a happy thing. It brings sadness, stress, and challenge to both the person experiencing it and his or her loved ones. It isn't all bad, either. The person with dementia is still God's child and is still a human person. And it may be helpful for us to recognize in that person some of the innocence of and feelings we have for a beloved child. A wise Jesuit priest, Rev. Carl Dehne, SJ, mentioned on page 13, has emphasized two points to me: People with dementia still have feelings, even if they can't express them; and don't be condescending with them. For a long time I didn't give the topic much thought. I felt bad for those experiencing dementia and those who love them, and I found (and still find) those supposedly funny e-mail blasts about forgetful seniors distasteful at best. But dementia wasn't within my range of immediate experience. And then, within the past year, three people I know, love, and cherish were diagnosed with the onset of Alzheimer's. All are bright, kind, caring people. And all (I did not expect this) were younger than I am. Dementia became very real and very personal to me, as it already is for so many others. And now it has become part of my prayers for difficult times. The prayers are day by day, of course, since life is day by day. But here is one of them.

❊ Forgetting and Sometimes Forgotten

O, Lord of Mental Acuity, you are the universal parent of us all. Hold in your cosmic care all who suffer or will suffer from dementia. Grant that they will be cared for and cared about as needed and deserved. And guide us—as individuals, family, friends, and society—to help them find what help they need to continue to experience the beauty of your creation. Help them find peace and comfort and a sense of your loving presence. I don't believe that your all-embracing all-enduring love is too small to reach them. And while you're at it, Parent God, help the rest of us to reflect on the way we react and respond to those with dementia. Give all who care directly for them wisdom, strength, courage—and the support they need from the rest of us. Let us react to them as we would want them to react to us.

> *"Look around you: Winter is over;*
> *the winter rains are over, gone!*
> *Spring flowers are in blossom all over.*
> *The whole world's a choir—and singing!*
> *Spring warblers are filling the forest*
> *with sweet arpeggios.*
> *Lilacs are exuberantly purple and perfumed,*
> *and cherry trees fragrant with blossoms."*
> *(Song of Songs 2:11-13)*

❊ My Prayers and Scriptures

PART FOUR

Prayers for
Moving Forward

TIMES OF GROWTH, DISCIPLESHIP, RELATIONSHIP, SIGHING, AGING, FORGIVING, JOY, REMEMBERING, AND TRANSITION

"Prayer is neither black magic nor is it a form of demand note. Prayer is a relationship." I found this in a book called *Nightlight,* by John Huess. It is one of my all-time favorite descriptions of prayer. So simply and elegantly stated, but not all simple to do. Words can all too easily become mechanical. This is one of the reasons for praying, and writing down your own prayers, as you were asked to do at the end of each section in this book. It is a reminder that you are not reciting words but *speaking* and *hearing* words—words to and from Someone who wants to hear specifically from you, words to and from Someone who waits to answer you. What follows are a dozen or so more of my prayers. I pray for different reasons and for no reason at all. I don't pray as often as I should or want, but when I do it always brings me comfort. I have focused in this book on the "difficult" times of life, but life is not always difficult, so I have snuck a few prayers for "easy" times in here as well. I end by praying for my own "ultimate transition," and I ask that you do the same. I'll meet you on the other side. Amen.

❀ Letting Go, Not Giving Up

God of Transitions, help me to let go of trying to live "Life as It Should Be According to My Divine Plan for the Universe." Help me instead to work on trying to live "Life as It Should Be According to Your Divine Plan for the Universe." Lord of Illumination, shed your light on the sometimes rocky path to my being better, wiser, kinder—so that life can become as it should be for all your children, all your creatures, and your entire universe.

> *God rises on you,*
> *his sunrise glory breaks over you. (Isaiah 60:2)*

※ Growing Where I'm Planted

Sometimes, actually most times, I don't know where I fit in your garden, God of Growing Things. Some people seem to live and grow where they're planted, wherever that is at the time. Not so me. Not often enough anyway. Because how and/or where should I be planted so I can grow? Am I planted deep enough? Not too deep or too shallow? Shouldn't I be just a few feet, or a few hundred or thousand miles, in this direction or that? So how then do I know where to plant myself in order to grow and become part of your garden, Lord of Life?

> ***"But blessed is the man who trusts me, God,***
> ***the woman who sticks with God.***
> ***They're like trees replanted in Eden,***
> ***putting down roots near the rivers—***
> ***Never a worry through the hottest of summers,***
> ***never dropping a leaf,***
> ***Serene and calm through droughts,***
> ***bearing fresh fruit every season." (Jeremiah 17:7-8)***

※ Wanted: Wisdom Figure

Where do I look for wisdom, Wise Lord, now that I am supposed to be the adult in my life? I thought that by now I would be so much smarter—or at least further along the way—with all this experience behind me. But then I think of all the things I've done and left undone, all the people I've known or didn't choose to know. It's not that I want someone to tell me what to do—heaven forbid! It's just that it would be really handy to have a wisdom figure that would sometimes—not always—turn out to be *me!* Help me to grow in mature wisdom and compassion, God of Both of Them. For myself. For others. Yet still let me keep my inner child, the one who plays, who wonders, who learns.

> ***Jesus matured, growing up in both body and spirit, blessed by both God and people. (Luke 2:52)***

❀ R.S.V.P.—Sort of

Lord Who Calls Us, I want to answer your call. I want to draw near to you, to reach for your hand. But maybe I don't want to draw too near, at least right now. This is not out of indifference; it is out of my fear and anxiety. To tell the truth, I'm a little afraid of drawing near. When I think of what happened to your Son's first disciples, I get scared. I know trying to do the right thing can have its difficulties. All right, doing the wrong thing has its own problems. I've learned that too. But still, how can I ask you to keep me at a distance and still call myself your Son's disciple? Help me draw near to him and learn from him in order to best serve you, God with a Plan for Everyone. Help me take courage and comfort in your call.

> *David continued to address Solomon: "Take charge! Take heart! Don't be anxious or get discouraged. God, my God, is with you in this; he won't walk off and leave you in the lurch. He's at your side until every last detail is completed for conducting the worship of God." (1 Chronicles 28:20)*

❀ Guilty Plea

Lord of Judgment, there is no weaseling on this one. I did it. I said it. I'm flat-out, no contest wrong. And other people were hurt. If I could take it back, would I? If I could undo it, redo it, would I? In a New York minute. But that minute is gone, at least this time. So here now is my prayer: help me to make amends, God of Reconciliation, where I can, and help me do better next time so I don't have to say another prayer quite like this again soon.

> *God is fair and just;*
> *He corrects the misdirected,*
> *Sends them in the right direction.*
> *He gives the rejects his hand. (Psalm 25:8-9)*

✽ Real Age

Timeless God, you and I both know the truth about my real age, even if others don't recognize it. And the truth is that inside I'm forever roughly twenty-four, not the age that ridiculous paperwork like my birth certificate says. It's not that I don't respect older people or appreciate the perspective of experience—and, yes, wit and wisdom—age can bring. I do. I'm one of them! But being old should be a stage, not a disgrace. I object personally to growing old, even gracefully (which you may have already noted I haven't accomplished very well so far anyway). On the other hand, I'd like to postpone, at least for now, the alternative. So is there any chance, Lord of No Age at All, that together we could work out a package agreement where you help me keep on growing, without growing into what I consider "old" age?

> *When I was an infant at my mother's breast, I gurgled and cooed like any infant. When I grew up, I left those infant ways for good. (1 Corinthians 13:11)*

✽ Second-Hand Problems

God of Good Counsel, sometimes I feel beset by second-hand problems. So many of the people I care about—that you care about—face so many difficulties: relationships, finances, health, career, personal transformations, societal transitions. I think about it, worry about it, sometimes want to forget about it, and yet I still want to help. Yet sometimes I feel guilty that I can't, or don't know how, to help. Do you ever feel that way, Lord Who Has It All Together? Help me know how and when to join in the helping.

> *Never walk away from someone who deserves help;*
> *your hand is God's hand for that person.*
> *Don't tell your neighbor "Maybe some other time"*
> *or "Try me tomorrow" when the money's*
> *right there in your pocket. (Proverbs 3:27-28)*

❋ Reminder to Remember

Lord of Remembering, I don't think I'm ever tempted to think of myself as saintly. I have plenty of other temptations, but not that one. If I ever am so tempted, I bring myself back to earth by recalling examples of the people who really are saintly—but don't know it. The woman who cleans at my former exercise club, for example. She is a widow, who works two jobs, cares with devotion for her mother-in-law, and has offered to bring me a dual-language Bible, like hers, because she knows I am working on my Spanish. Help me, God of All Saints, to notice—and to learn—from the quiet examples of others.

> *Many women have done wonderful things,*
> *but you've outclassed them all!*
> *Charm can mislead and beauty soon fades.*
> *The woman to be admired and praised*
> *is the woman who lives in the Fear-of-God.*
> *Give her everything she deserves!*
> *Festoon her life with praises! (Proverbs 31:29-31)*

❋ Quiet Joy

This is a time of quiet joy for me, God of Difficult Times. Some might call it just "contentment," and that would be correct as well. It's nothing big—the reasons for my joy, I mean. In fact, I'm not even sure why I feel it. Perhaps I could think of a dozen reasons, or maybe nothing I can identify. Never mind, Lord of All Reasons and None at All. For this moment, I just want to thank you—quietly, calmly, joyfully—for being with me in all my difficult times.

> *"I'm bursting with God-news;*
> *I'm dancing the song of my Savior God.*
> *God took one good look at me, and look what happened—*
> *I'm the most fortunate woman on earth!" (Luke 1:47-48)*

❈ Today and Tomorrow and Yesterday

Once again, Unchanging Lord, this is a time of transition for me.
There seem to be a lot of them—these times in-between. Waiting and
worrying about something that will—or could—happen. Recovering and
remembering something that did happen. Looking forward to something
that might or might not happen. And then without noticing, God of
Constant Surprises, the todays and tomorrows have somehow slipped away
and become yesterdays, and all my good intentions have gone to the land of
good intentions. Help me live one day at a time, until I have none left.

*We don't yet see things clearly. We're squinting in a fog, peering
through a mist. But it won't be long before the weather clears and
the sun shines bright! We'll see it all then, see it all as clearly as
God sees us, knowing him directly just as he knows us!*
(1 Corinthians 13:12)

❈ Here I Am, Lord...Still

I don't consider myself old, Timeless God, but I'm not getting any younger
either! So when do I decide that I'm entitled to step back and just rest or
play, and when should I remember there is much work yet to be done in
building the City of God in the here and now? I still want to contribute to
the common good, but goofing off has more and more attraction these days.
Help me strike some kind of balance, Lord of Heaven and Earth, between
having a life and giving back to life. Maybe it is doing both that will create
the balance I crave.

And then I heard the voice of the Master
   "Whom shall I send?
   Who will go for us?"
I spoke up,
   "I'll go.
   Send me!" (Isaiah 6:8)

✼ Admitting the (Small) Faults

Forgiving Lord, there are a lot of my faults I don't mind all that much admitting. In fact, I might as well admit them, since everyone else has probably already noticed them anyway. But the ones I don't like to admit are all the petty little feelings that can lead to petty perspectives and, worse, petty behaviors and words on my part. Shouldn't I have grown more out of this by now? But it's one thing to acknowledge being a sinner and quite another to count all the ways I am a flawed human being. I count on you, God of No Excuses, to help me grow day by day, even if it's in small (not petty) ways.

> *But for right now, friends, I'm completely frustrated by your un-spiritual dealings with each other and with God. You're acting like infants in relation to Christ, capable of nothing much more than nursing at the breast. Well, then, I'll nurse you since you don't seem capable of anything more. As long as you grab for what makes you feel good or makes you look important, are you really much different than a babe at the breast, content only when everything's going your way? (1 Corinthians 3:1-3)*

The Ultimate Transition

Lord of Journeys, one day, some day, I know I will come face to face with the transition of transitions. And I hope I will come face to face with you, in an embrace like no other. I admit I find the whole idea of my own death a bit scary. Not just the Departure but the Arrival! You better than anyone, God of Mercy, know how far from perfect I am, so I'm depending on your amazing grace: "How sweet the sound!" In the meantime, let me live so that when my Departure comes I will not only Arrive somewhere better, but the world, this world, will be at least a little better because I was here. I end this prayer, Lord of My Life, with one of my favorite Persian proverbs. I'm sure you have heard it many times: "We come into this world crying while all around us are smiling. May we so live that we go out of this world smiling while all around us are weeping."

> ***For right now, until that completeness, we have three things to do to lead us toward that consummation: Trust steadily in God, hope unswervingly, love extravagantly. And the best of the three is love. (1 Corinthians 13:13)***

✽ My Prayers and Scriptures

❈ My Prayers and Scriptures

❊ My Prayers and Scriptures

❋ My Prayers and Scriptures

Prayer Index

Scripture Index

About the Author

Helen Reichert Lambin has been writing practical books on scripture, theology, grief, and prayer for over thirty years for ACTA Publications.

She is especially known for her best-selling book *The Death of a Husband*, which broke new ground for books on grief because of its honesty, transparency, and insight into the realities of widowhood.

Her most recent books include *Prayers for Sleepless Nights* and *Constructing a New Normal*. She is presently working on a new book on the death of a sibling or close friend or relative.

Now in her eighties, Helen lives in Chicago, where she enjoys her children, granddaughter, and grandpets. Because of her many tattoos (all done since she turned seventy), Helen is known in the local media as "the tattooed grandma of Edgewater."

Books by Helen Reichert Lambin

CONSTRUCTING A NEW NORMAL
Dealing Effectively with Losses Throughout Life

Helen Lambin addresses a wide variety of experiences of grief and transition with grace, courage, tongue-in-cheek humor, and a love for the riches of language and the power of metaphor. 160 pages, paperback

PRAYERS FOR SLEEPLESS NIGHTS

While this collection of practical prayers may not help readers actually fall asleep, it will give them a framework to do something constructive: create a personal relationship with God. 80 pages, paperback

THE DEATH OF HUSBAND
Reflections for a Grieving Wife

Forty reflections on different facets of the grieving process offer insights will touch a woman's heart, heal her soul, and point out new and hopeful directions. 128 pages, paperback

Also Available

THE MESSAGE
Catholic/Ecumenical Edition

A fresh, compelling, insightful, challenging, faith-filled translation of the Bible into contemporary idiomatic American English. 1,984 pages, paperback and hardcover

**Available from booksellers
or from ACTA Publications
www.actapublications • 800-397-2282**